WESTERN ISLES LIBRARIES

Readers are requested to take great care of the item while in their possession, and to point out any defects that they may notice in them to the Librarian.
This item should be returned on or before the latest date stamped below, but an extension of the period of loan may be granted when desired.

DATE OF RETURN	DATE OF RETURN	DATE OF RETURN
2 5 MAR 2011		

Heinemann
LIBRARY

www.heinemann.co.uk/library
Visit our website to find out more information about Heinemann Library books.

To order:
☎ Phone 44 (0)1865 888066
▤ Send a fax to 44 (0)1865 314091
▣ Visit the Heinemann Library Bookshop at www.heinemann.co.uk/library to browse our catalogue and order online.

First published in Great Britain by Heinemann Library, Halley Court, Jordan Hill, Oxford OX2 8EJ, part of Pearson Education. Heinemann Library is a registered trademark of Pearson Education Ltd.

© Pearson Education Ltd 2007
First published in paperback in 2008
The moral right of the proprietor has been asserted.

Editorial: Joanna Talbot
Design: Kimberly R. Miracle, Fiona MacColl and Ray Hendren
Illustrations: Cavedweller Studios
Picture Research: Melissa Allison
Production: Duncan Gilbert

We would like to thank Nigel Saunders for his assistance in the preparation of this book.

Originated by Dot Gradations Ltd
Printed and bound in China by Leo Paper Group

ISBN 978 0 431 04029 5 (hardback)
11 10 09 08 07
10 9 8 7 6 5 4 3 2 1

ISBN 978 0 431 04035 6 (paperback)
12 11 10 09 08
10 9 8 7 6 5 4 3 2 1

British Library Cataloguing in Publication Data
Halls, Kelly Milner, 1957-
Forces and motion. - (Science projects)
1. Force and energy - Juvenile literature 2. Motion - Juvenile literature 3. Force and energy - Experiments - Juvenile literature 4. Motion - Experiments - Juvenile literature
I. Title
531.6

Acknowledgements
The author and publishers are grateful to the following for permission to reproduce copyright material: Alamy/OnRequest Images.Inc, p. **16**; Corbis, pp. **28** (Duomo), **32** (Lew Robertson), **36** (Macduff Everton), **46**; Courtesy of Antibubble.com, p. **40**; Getty Images, pp. **6**, **8** (Image Bank), **12**, **39**, **20** (Photodisc), **15** (Hulton Archive), **24** (Stone); Masterfile/Andrew Douglas, p. **4**.

Cover photograph reproduced with permission of Masterfile Royalty-free. Background image from istockphoto.com. Car illustration by istockphoto.com/ Brian Sullivan

Every effort has been made to contact copyright holders of any material reproduced in this book. Any omissions will be rectified in subsequent printings if notice is given to the publishers.

Disclaimer

Contents

» Some words are shown in bold, **like this**. You can find the definitions for these words in the glossary.

Starting your science investigation

A science investigation is an exciting challenge. It starts with an idea that you can test by doing experiments. These are often lots of fun to do. But it is no good just charging in without planning first. A good scientist knows that they must first research their idea thoroughly, work out how they can test it, and plan their experiments carefully. When they have done these things, they can happily carry out their experiments to see if their idea is right.

Your experiments might support your original idea or they might shoot it down in flames. This doesn't matter. The important thing is that you will have found out a bit more about the world around you, and had fun along the way. You will be a happy scientist!

In this book, you'll look at nine science investigations involving forces and motion. You'll be able to discover some wonderful things about the world you live in.

Do your research

Is there something about forces and motion that you've always wondered about? Something you don't quite understand but would like to? Then do a little research about the subject. Go to the library and find some books about the subject. Books written for students are often a very good place to start.

Use your favourite Internet search engine to find reliable online resources. Websites written by museums, universities, newspapers and scientific journals are among the best sources for accurate research. Each investigation in this book has some suggestions for further research.

You need to make sure that your resources are reliable when doing research. Ask yourself the following questions, especially about the resources you find online.

The investigations

The start of each investigation contains a box like this.

Possible question

This question is a suggested starting point for your investigation. You will need to adapt the question to suit the things that interest you.

Materials needed

Make sure you can easily get all of the materials listed and gather them together before starting work.

Possible hypothesis

This is only a suggestion. Don't worry if your hypothesis doesn't match the one listed here. Use your imagination!

Level of difficulty

There are three levels of investigations in this book: Easy, Intermediate, and Advanced. The level of difficulty is based on how long the investigation takes and how complicated it is.

Approximate cost of materials

Discuss this with your parents before starting work. Don't spend too much.

1) How old is the resource? Is the information up to date or is it very old?

2) Who wrote the resource? Is the author identified so you know who they are, and what qualifies them to write about the topic?

3) What is the purpose of the resource? A website from a business or pressure group might not give balanced information, but one from a university probably will.

4) Is the information well documented? Can you tell where the author got their information from so you can check how accurate it is?

Some websites allow you to "chat" online with experts. Make sure you discuss this with a parent or teacher first. Never give out personal information online. The "Think U Know" website at http://www.thinkuknow.co.uk has loads of tips about safety online.

Once you know a little more about the subject you want to investigate, you'll be ready to work out your scientific question. You will be able to use this to make a sensible **hypothesis**. A hypothesis is an idea about why something happens that can be tested by doing experiments. Finally, you'll be ready to begin your science investigation!

What is an experiment?

Often when someone says that they are going to do an experiment, they mean they are just going to fiddle with something to see what happens. But scientists mean something else. They mean that they are going to control the **variables** involved in a careful way. A variable is something that changes or can be changed. **Independent variables** are things that you deliberately keep the same or change in your experiment. You should always aim to keep all the independent variables constant, except for the one you are investigating. The **dependent variable** is the change that happens because of the one independent variable that you do change. You make a fair test if you set up your experiment so that you only change one independent variable at a time. Your results are **valid** if you have carried out a fair test, and recorded your results or observations honestly.

Sometimes you might want to compare one group with another to see what happens. For example, if you wanted to show the effect of minerals on plants, you might use 10 potted plants. You would give five of them tap water only (Group A) and five of them liquid fertiliser (Group B). Group A is your **control** group and group B is your test group. You would be looking to see if there is a difference between the two groups. In this experiment, the liquid fertiliser is the independent variable, and the effect on the plant is the dependent variable.

What forces keep this roller coaster on its track?

You must do experiments carefully so that your results are **accurate** and **reliable**. Ideally, you would get the same results if you did your investigation all over again.

Your hypothesis

Once you've decided on the question you're going to try to answer, you then make a scientific **prediction** of what you'll find out in your science project.

For example, if you're interested in speed, your question might be "Which goes faster when it is pushed, a skateboard or a scooter?" Remember, a hypothesis is an idea about why something happens, which can be tested by doing experiments. So your hypothesis in response to the above question might be, "A skateboard will go faster because it is lighter, and lighter objects go faster when pushed." With a hypothesis, you can also work out if you can actually do the experiments needed to answer your question. Think of a question like: "Can everyone be taught to float in water?". It would be impossible to support your hypothesis, however you express it. This is because you can't possibly test everybody in the world. So, be sure you can actually get the **evidence** needed to support or disprove your hypothesis.

Keeping records

Good scientists keep careful notes in their lab book about everything they do. This is really important. Other scientists may want to try out the experiments to see if they get the same results. So the records in your lab book need to be clear and easy to follow. What sort of things should you write down?

It is a good idea to write some notes about the research you found in books and on websites. You should also include the names of the books or the web addresses. This will save you from having to find these useful resources all over again later. You should also write down your hypothesis and your reasons for it. All your **data** and results should go into your lab book, too.

Your results are the evidence that you use to make your conclusion. Never rub out an odd-looking result or tweak it to "look right". An odd result may turn out to be important later. You should write down *every* result you get. Tables are a really good way to record lots of results clearly. Make sure you record when you did your experiments, and anything you might have changed along the way to improve them. No detail is too small when it comes to scientific research.

There are tips for making a great report with each investigation and at the end of this book. Use them as guides and don't be afraid to be creative. Make it *your* investigation!

free fall

Gravity is a universal force. This means that it's everywhere and it affects everything. But does gravity have a bigger effect on bigger things? This investigation will help you understand a little more about gravity and its effects.

Do your research

This investigation looks at whether an object's size and **mass** affects how quickly it falls to the ground. Before you start your investigation, do some research on gravity to find out why objects fall. Once you've done this, you can tackle this investigation. Or, you might come up with your own idea for an investigation after you've learned more about gravity.

You could start your research with this book and these two websites:

» *Gravity (Fantastic Forces)*, Chris Oxlade (Heinemann Educational Books, 2006)

» Fear of physics:
  http://www.fearofphysics.com/Fall/fall.html

» skoool:
  http://kent.skoool.co.uk (then search for "gravity")

Background information

Possible question

Do size and mass affect the speed at which an object falls?

Possible hypothesis

Yes – large, heavy objects will fall faster than small, light objects.

Level of difficulty

Easy

Approximate cost of materials

Free

Materials needed

» Ten unbreakable objects from around the house. (**Check with a parent that it really is OK for you to drop these objects**.) Consider, for example, an empty plastic food container, a shoe, a book, a teddy bear, a pencil, a toothbrush, a tennis ball, a football, a hairbrush, and a coin.

» Kitchen scales (to find the **weight** of each object)

» A tape measure (to measure the drop height)

» A stopwatch (to time each drop)

» A ladder and an adult to keep it steady

» A partner to work the stopwatch

Outline of methods

1. List each of your objects in your lab book and record their shapes, sizes, and weights. Before you drop the objects, make some predictions in your lab book about how they will fall, including which object will fall fastest.

2. Set up your ladder on a flat surface outside. It needs to be next to a high wall, such as the side of a house. Make sure you keep away from any traffic. Assemble your objects at the bottom of the ladder.

3. Make sure your partner knows what to do with the stopwatch. They must start the stopwatch as soon as you let go of an object, and stop it as soon as the object hits the ground. They will have to watch carefully so that they time the drops **accurately**.

Continued

4. **Ask an adult to keep the ladder steady** and to hand you each object as you need it. Climb the ladder.

ADULT SUPERVISION NEEDED

5. Choose a part of the wall near to the top of the ladder. Use a piece of masking tape to mark the wall there. Hold the tape measure to the tape mark, and ask your partner to measure the length to the ground. Record the height in your lab book. You need to release each object from that point so that the results will be as reliable as possible.

Step 6

6. Hold an object in your hand and make sure your partner is ready with the stopwatch. Drop the object from your release point. Record in your lab book how long the object is in the air, from release to impact.

7. Repeat step 6 two more times with the same object. Take a good look at the three times. If one of them is very different from the other two, repeat step 6 again.

8. Work out the mean time for the recorded drops. You do this by adding the times together and dividing by the number of drops you did. Record this mean time in your lab book.

9. Repeat steps 6, 7, and 8 for each of the other objects.

Analysis of results

» Did the larger objects fall faster?

» Did the heavier objects fall faster?

» Looking at the results for each object in turn, were the three times about the same or did they vary a lot?

» Did anything go badly wrong in your experiments? And did anything go really well? Can you think of any way to make your experiments better?

More activities to extend your investigation

» Drop objects that are the same shape, but different weights. For example, you could drop a golf ball, a table tennis ball, and a squash ball. Drop them together.

» Change the drop height. Drop the items from higher or lower points on the ladder and compare the results.

Project extras

» Film your investigation or make a PowerPoint® presentation and show your class. Take photos to stick in your report.

Boing...boING...BOING

Gravity is an unusual force. The Earth's gravity is strong enough to stop you flying off into space. Yet you overcome it every time you lift your foot. This investigation, using four different balls of the same size, will help you find out why some objects bounce off the ground higher than others.

Do your research

A ball falls to the ground when it is dropped. Usually it bounces back up, only to be pulled back down again. This investigation looks at what affects how a ball bounces. You are going to use balls that are the same size but different **masses** and materials. Table tennis balls, squash balls, and golf balls are ideal because they are nearly identical in size. Before you start your investigation, do some research to find out about bouncing. Once you've done this, you can tackle this investigation. Or, you might come up with an idea of your own after you've learned more about the topic.

You could start your research with these two websites:

» Sport! science: That's the way the ball bounces:
   http://www.exploratorium.edu/sports/ball_bounces/index.html

» How things work – bouncing balls:
   http://howthingswork.virginia.edu/bouncing_balls.html

Background information

Possible question

Do same-sized balls with different masses bounce to the same height?

Possible hypothesis

Balls with a low mass will not bounce as high as balls with a greater mass.

Level of difficulty

Easy

Approximate cost of materials

£6.00

Materials needed

» A table tennis ball and a golf ball. Two different squash balls (look for ones with different coloured spots, for example yellow, green, or red).
» Masking tape and a marker pen
» Kitchen scales (to weigh the balls)
» A tape measure (to measure the bounce height)
» A ladder and an adult to steady it
» A partner to mark where the balls bounce

Outline of methods

1. Weigh each of the balls and record their weight in your lab book.

2. Set up your ladder on a flat surface such as a driveway or school playground. Your ladder needs to be next to a high wall such as the side of a house. Make sure you keep away from any traffic.

3. Ask your partner to stand about a metre away, facing the wall. They need to be able to keep a close eye on where the ball bounces.

4. **ADULT SUPERVISION NEEDED** **Ask an adult to keep the ladder steady each time you climb it.** Climb the ladder.

5. Choose a part of the wall near to the top of the ladder and in easy reach. Use a piece of masking tape to mark the wall there.

6. Use the tape measure to find the height of your mark from the ground. Record this height in your lab note book. You will use this height for all four balls.

Continued

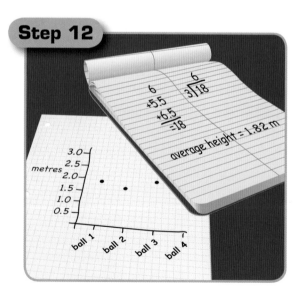

7. Drop the first ball from the top of your ladder at the height you measured. Make sure you drop the ball from this exact, measured point as your partner watches. **Do not** put any force behind the drop. Just let go of the ball. This way, your results will reflect what the ball does naturally, not what your muscle power can make it do.

8. Ask your partner to mark the wall with a piece of masking tape at the point where the ball bounced the highest. If your assistant missed the drop, or wasn't sure how high it bounced, do the drop again.

9. Repeat steps 7 and 8 twice more with the same ball. Each time ask your partner to mark the wall with a piece of masking tape at the point where the ball bounced the highest. Ask them to label each piece "1st try", "2nd try" and "3rd try" as appropriate.

10. Measure the height of each try and record all of the **data** in your lab book.

11. Remove all the masking tape and repeat steps 7 to 10 using another ball. Do this for all four balls.

12. Work out the mean height that each ball bounced. You do this by adding the three heights for a ball together, then dividing by three. Record the mean bounce heights in your lab book.

Analysis of results

» Did all the balls bounce at the same height, even though they had different masses?

» Did the material the balls were made from affect the results?

» How would your results change if you dropped the balls from a lower height?

More activities to extend your investigation

» Let each ball bounce more than once. Record their second, third, and fourth bounces as well as their first one. Draw a bar chart to show your results. Do the bounces decrease in height by the same amount each time? Do some balls keep bouncing higher than others?

» Warm one of the squash balls up in some hot water. Does it bounce higher or lower than before? What happens if you bounce the ball after chilling it in the fridge or freezer?

Project extras

» Film your experiments to show your class. If you have a digital camera that can take lots of photos quickly one after the other, photograph a ball falling and bouncing back up. Glue the sequence of photos into your report.

Sir Isaac Newton is often said to have discovered gravity. Did he really discover it or was it there already?

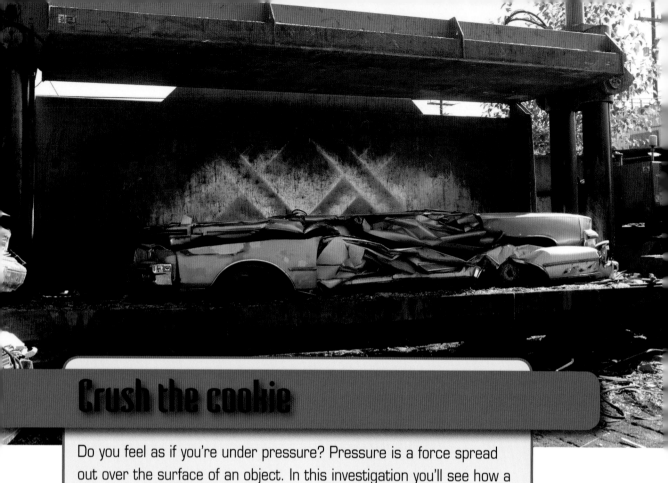

Crush the cookie

Do you feel as if you're under pressure? Pressure is a force spread out over the surface of an object. In this investigation you'll see how a little pressure can go a long way.

Do your research

This investigation looks at **gravity**, **mass** and force. You are going to have a go at crushing Chinese fortune cookies. Before you start, do some research on the different forces in nature. Once you've done this, you can tackle this investigation. Or, you may come up with an idea of your own after you've read and learned more about forces.

You could start your research with these two websites:

» skoool:

http://kent.skoool.co.uk (then search for "forces")

» Chinese fortune cookies recipe:

http://www.asianonlinerecipes.com/desserts/chinese_fortune_cookies.php

Background information

Possible question

How much force does it take to break a fortune cookie?

Possible hypothesis

A fortune cookie will break when a force of 5 **Newtons** is applied to it.

Level of difficulty

Easy

Approximate cost of materials

£2.00 + coins

Materials Needed

» Three fortune cookies (from some supermarkets or a Chinese restaurant, or make your own)
» One sheet of clear, flexible plastic
» One small piece of cardboard
» 100 2p coins
» A pair of scissors
» Sticky tape
» A ruler

Outline of methods

Step 2

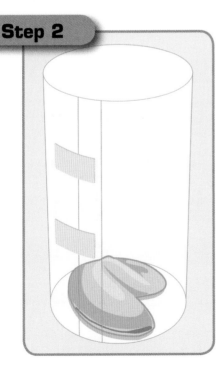

1. Measure the length of your fortune cookie, from end to end, with the ruler. Record this in your lab book.

2. Roll your sheet of plastic into a tube just wide enough to allow the cookie to sit flat inside it.

3. Measure the **diameter** of the open end of your tube and record that **data** in your lab book.

4. Cut a circle of cardboard with the same diameter as the tube. Tape the circle securely over one end of the tube. This will be the bottom of your tube.

Continued

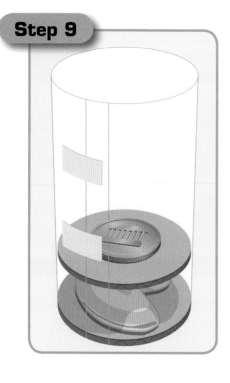

Step 9

5. Stand the tube upright on a flat surface, such as a kitchen table.

6. Slip the fortune cookie into the tube so it rests on the cardboard bottom.

7. Cut a second circle of cardboard about 4 mm less than the diameter of the bottom of your tube. It should fit snugly inside the tube, on top of the fortune cookie.

8. Gather your coins together. A 2p piece has a mass of 7.12 g. This means that it weighs 0.0712 newtons (N). You can use 1p pieces instead, but a 1p piece is exactly half the weight of a 2p piece, so you will need twice as many.

9. Put a 2p piece into the tube on the top cardboard circle. Look through the gap in the tube for any sign that the cookie might be breaking.

10. Repeat step 9, adding one coin at a time, until part of the cookie breaks. Write down in your lab book the number of coins it took to cause the first break in the cookie.

11. Keep adding coins until you run out of coins or the cookie is completely crushed under their weight. Make careful notes in your lab book each time part of the cookie breaks. Write down which part broke and under how many coins.

12. Work out the total weight of coins needed to make the first break, and to crush the cookie completely. If you used 2p coins, the total weight in N is the number of coins multiplied by 0.0712. If you used 1p coins, multiply the number of coins by 0.0356 instead.

13. Repeat the experiment two more times to check the reliability of your data. Work out the mean weight needed to break the cookie. To do this, add together your three results, then divide by three.

Analysis of results

» Did the cookie break sooner or later than you expected?

» How **reliable** were your results? Did different cookies break at about the same weight, or did they vary a lot?

» Do you think the results would have changed if you'd put in more than one coin at a time?

» Do you think other kinds of cookie or biscuit would hold up better?

More activities to extend your investigation

» Repeat the experiment, but stand the cookie on one end in the tube using Blu Tack® or Plasticene®.

» Repeat the experiment using "flying saucer" sweets and compare your data.

» Repeat the experiment but put 10 coins in at a time instead of one.

» Repeat the experiment putting in 25 coins at a time, and compare the results.

» See if it makes a difference if you drop each coin from a specific height above the tube, instead of placing them inside.

Project extras

» Examine the broken fortune cookies carefully. Did they all break at the same point? Examine the broken part using a microscope. Take photos through the microscope if you can. Ask a teacher to help you.

» Weigh a fortune cookie. How many more times its own weight was needed to break it?

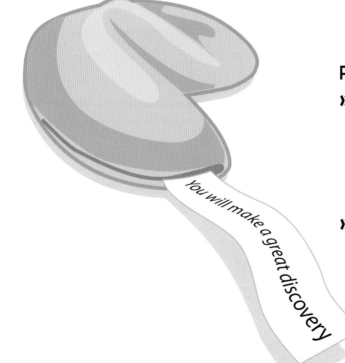

You will make a great discovery

fly, paper, fly!

When something flies, we sometimes say it "defies **gravity**," as if it stops gravity pulling it down to the ground. But that's not really true. Flying uses gravity, speed, and lift to make things happen that might seem like magic. People who design and build aeroplanes know that the materials used in their construction make a big difference to their flying success. This investigation uses paper aeroplanes to help show how important this is.

Do your research

This investigation looks at flight and how different materials affect an object's ability to fly. Before you start your investigation, do some research to find out more about flight, **aerodynamics**, aeroplanes, and what materials are used to make them. Once you've done some research, you can tackle this investigation. Or, you may come up with an idea of your own after you've read and learned more about the topic.

You could start your research with this book and website:

» *Super Simple Paper Airplanes*, Nick Robinson (Sterling Publishing, 2005)
» Ken Blackburn's Paper Airplanes:
   http://www.paperplane.org

Background information

Possible question

Does the kind of paper used change how a paper aeroplane flies?

Possible hypothesis

No – the aeroplane will fly the same way, no matter what paper it's made of.

Level of difficulty	Approximate cost of materials
Easy	£1.00

Materials needed

Note: The thickness of paper and card is measured in grams per square metre (written as gsm by paper makers). The bigger the number, the thicker the paper.

» One sheet of A4 thin file paper
» One sheet of A4 thick typing paper
» One sheet of A4 card
» Paper aeroplane template
» Tape measure (to measure the distance flown by your aeroplane)

Outline of methods

1. Use an A4 sheet for each aeroplane. If you don't know the thickness in gsm, you might want to weigh each sheet instead and record the results in your lab book.

2. Fold each of your sheets of paper into the same type of paper aeroplane. Use the template pictured right and the diagrams over the page to help you.

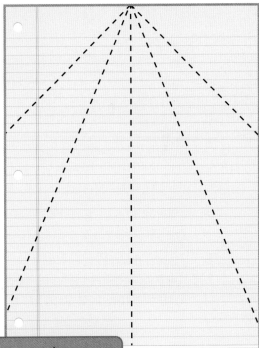

This is one paper aeroplane template but you can find many others. See the diagrams over the page to find out how to fold it.

Continued

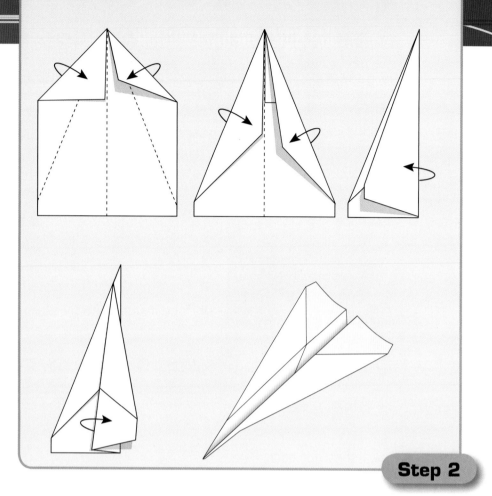

3. Go outside and mark a spot on the ground to be your launch pad.

4. The aim is to set off each aeroplane using exactly the same movements and speed, in exactly the same direction. You must try to make each launch identical to the last, so choose a calm day.

5. Launch one of your aeroplanes. Measure the distance of the flight from launch to landing. Record the **data** in your lab book.

6. Repeat step 5 four more times with the same aeroplane. Work out the mean distance flown and record it in your lab book. To do this, add together the distances of all five flights, then divide by five.

7. Repeat steps 5 and 6 for each of your paper aeroplanes and record all of the results in your lab book.

8. Plot a bar chart to show the mean distance flown by all your aeroplanes. This will let you compare the different types of paper used.

Analysis of results

» How **reliable** were your results? Did the same aeroplane always fly exactly the same distance?

» Which aeroplane flew the furthest?

» Were the results what you expected?

» Is there a trend in your data? For example, do the aeroplanes fly further the heavier they are?

» If you were outside, how did weather conditions affect the flight of your aeroplanes?

» What other factors might have affected the flight of your aeroplanes?

More activities to extend your investigation

» Add a paper clip to the nose of each aeroplane and see if that affects how far they fly.

» Add a vertical tail to each aeroplane and see if that affects how far they fly.

» Investigate whether bending the back of each wing up or down affects how far the aeroplanes fly.

» Try the investigation indoors in a hall or other large room.

Project extras

» Take photos of your three aeroplanes and stick them in your report next to your findings for each one. Make a mobile from your aeroplanes to display in your classroom.

Parachute to safety

Leonardo da Vinci was an Italian artist and inventor. He sketched a design for a parachute in the 15th century. Da Vinci never did find out if his parachute worked. But a British parachutist, Adrian Nicholas, made one and successfully tested it in 2000. Da Vinci's parachute was shaped like a pyramid, but modern ones are not. This investigation will help you find out if the shape of a parachute matters.

Do your research

This investigation looks at the effect that the shape of a parachute has on **air resistance**. **Gravity** pulls objects down to the ground. Air resistance acts against gravity to slow down a falling object. Before you begin your project, do some research to find out about gravity, air resistance and balanced forces, as well as parachutes. Then you can tackle this investigation. Or, you may come up with an idea of your own after you've learned more about the topic.

Here are two websites you could start with for your research:

» British Library online gallery – Leonardo da Vinci:
http://www.bl.uk/onlinegallery/features/leonardo/leonardo.html
» Ranger Danger Dan: Interactive parachute simulation game:
http://puzzling.caret.cam.ac.uk/pregame.php?game=9

Background information

Possible question

Does the shape of a parachute affect how quickly it falls?

Possible hypothesis

The shape of a parachute will affect how quickly it falls because there will be different amounts of air resistance.

Level of difficulty

Intermediate

Approximate cost of materials

Free to £2.00

Materials needed

» Plastic carrier bags or plastic dustbin liners
» Scissors (to cut the plastic into shapes for the parachutes)
» String or cotton thread
» Small plastic figures, such as toy soldiers, about 2 to 5 cm tall. Try to make sure that they are the same size, shape and weight.
» A stopwatch (to time each drop)
» A ladder with an adult to keep it steady
» A partner to work the stopwatch

Outline of methods

1. Make five different parachutes for your toy figures using the plastic bags. Change either the shape of the parachute, or its area. If you change the shape, keep its area the same. And if you change the area, keep its size the same. Use the string to join the corners of each parachute to the toy.

Step 1

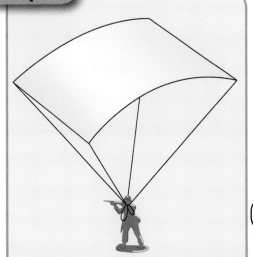

Continued

2. **Ask an adult to keep the ladder steady.** Climb the ladder.

ADULT SUPERVISION NEEDED

3. Put a piece of masking tape on the wall in easy reach. You will drop all your parachutes from this same point.

4. Ask your partner to hand you your first toy with its parachute. Make sure your partner is ready to time how long it takes for the parachute to reach the ground after being dropped.

5. Drop your first parachute and record the time in your lab book. Test the parachute at least two more times.

6. Repeat steps 4 and 5 for each of the other parachutes.

7. Work out the mean drop time for each parachute. You do this by adding the times together and dividing by the number of drops you did. Draw a bar chart of your mean drop times.

Analysis of results

» Does the shape or size make a difference in how successfully a parachute performs?

» Which shape or size of parachute fell the slowest and which fell the fastest? Did your results match your predictions?

» Based on your results, which parachute would you say is the safest? Why?

More activities to extend your investigation

» Does it make a difference how far the parachute falls? Try dropping your parachutes out of a first floor window to the garden below. **Make sure an adult is there for safety**.

» Try using heavier objects, such as a teddy bear.

» Investigate the effect of using different materials to make your parachutes. Try paper, thick plastic, aluminium cooking foil, and clothing material.

» Modern parachutes often have holes in them. Research why they are there. Investigate the effect of changing the size of the hole on the time taken for a parachute to fall.

Project extras

Make a PowerPoint® presentation or film of your investigation to show your class. Take photos to stick in your report.

Ramp up for speed

The ancient Egyptians used ramps to raise huge slabs of stone so they could make their pyramids. But it was hard and dangerous work. If the ropes holding a slab broke, it could slide back down the ramp. In this investigation you will find out how the angle of a ramp affects how fast an object moves down it.

Do your research

This investigation looks at **gravity** and **acceleration**. Gravity pulls an object down a ramp and makes it accelerate (speed up). Before you start your investigation, do some research on ramps. It might help to know that ramps are also called inclined planes. Once you've done this, you can tackle this investigation. Or, you might come up with an idea of your own after you've learned more about the topic.

Here are two websites you could start with for your research:

» Simple machines activities:

http://www.edheads.org/activities/simple%2Dmachines/

» Inclined plane simulation:

http://www.ngsir.netfirms.com/englishhtm/Incline.htm

Background information

Possible question

How much does the steepness of a ramp affect the speed of a toy car?

Possible hypothesis

Making the ramp steeper will make the car go faster because it is higher up.

Level of difficulty

Easy

Approximate cost of materials

£3.00

Materials needed

» One piece of planed wood, about 1 m long and at least 15 cm wide. Do not use "sawn" wood because this is too rough. You could also use a sheet of plywood or MDF for your ramp, but this will be more expensive.

» Books to change the steepness of the ramp (the angle of incline)

» A protractor (to measure the angle of incline)

» A toy car

» A stopwatch and a partner (to time the car)

Outline of methods

1. Put two books on the floor. Lay the wood on them to make a ramp. Measure the angle of incline (the angle of the ramp from the floor) using the protractor. Record it in your lab book.

Step 1

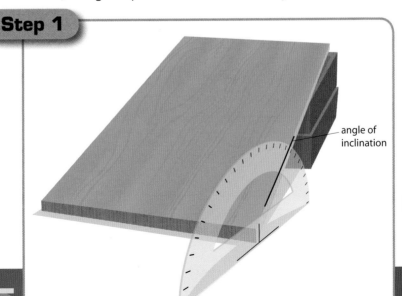

angle of inclination

Continued

2. If you are experimenting indoors, make sure you put a cushion just beyond the end of the ramp. This will stop the toy car rolling into the furniture and causing damage.

3. Hold the toy car at the top of the ramp and let it go without pushing it. Give your partner the stopwatch. Ask them to time the car from the moment you let go to the moment it reaches the floor at the end of the ramp. Record this time in your lab book.

4. Repeat step 3 two more times. Work out the mean time by adding the three times together and dividing by three. Record this mean time in your lab book.

5. Make the ramp steeper by adding more books. Measure its new angle of incline. Record this in your lab book.

6. Repeat steps 3 to 5 until you have done a range of experiments from a very shallow ramp to a very steep ramp.

Analysis of results

» Draw a graph with your mean times on the vertical axis and the angles of incline on the horizontal axis. What happened to the times as the angle of incline increased?

More activities to extend your investigation

» Find out the smallest angle of incline needed to get the car moving. What stops the car moving at smaller angles than this?

» Repeat your experiments, but this time measure the height of the top of the ramp from the floor. What differences, if any, do you find in your results?

» Repeat your experiments with different toy cars and compare your results with the first experiments. What difference, if any, does changing the weight or size of the car have?

» Put a spot of wet, washable poster paint on each back wheel. Put newspaper down at the end of the ramp, then let the car roll down it. It will leave little spots of paint on the ramp (not on the carpet!) as it goes. What do you notice about the distances between each spot of paint on the ramp?

» Visit a skateboard park and study which ramps seem to help skateboarders go the fastest.

Project extras

» Film your investigation or make a PowerPoint® presentation to show your class. Take photos to stick in your report.

You nailed it!

When an object is put into water it pushes, or displaces, some of the water. The object will float unless the weight of the displaced water is less than the weight of the object. As simple as it sounds, this idea helps people design life rafts, boats, and ships. In this investigation you will find out how changing the weight of an object affects its ability to float in water.

Do your research

This investigation looks at floating and sinking. Before you begin your investigation do some research to find out more about **buoyancy**, floating, and water. Once you've done this, you can tackle this investigation. Or, you might come up with an idea of your own after you've learned more about the topic.

Here are three websites you could start with for your research:

» How do life jackets work?: http://www.boatsafe.com/kids/pfdfloat.htm

» Nova online: Buoyancy basics:
   http://www.pbs.org/wgbh/nova/lasalle/buoybasics.html

» How objects float in fluids:
   http://www.school-for-champions.com/science/fluidfloating.htm

Background information

Possible question

Can nails sink a sponge?

Possible hypothesis

Sponges normally float in water, but adding too much weight will make them sink.

Level of difficulty

Easy

Approximate cost of materials

£4.00

Materials needed

» One small, dry household sponge
» One 200 g pack of 25 mm panel pins. DIY stores sell these nails.
» A large bucket or washing up bowl
» A towel (to dry your hands and the working area)
» Kitchen scales (to find the weight of the nails and sponge)
» Ruler (to measure how high the sponge floats)

Outline of methods

1. Weigh the sponge. Record this **data** in your lab book.

2. Fill the bucket or bowl with water until it is about three-quarters full.

3. Put the dry sponge into the water. Leave it for one minute then carefully measure and record how much of the sponge is floating above the water.

Step 3

Continued

4. Wet your sponge to make it soft. Squeeze out the excess water so that the sponge is damp, but not dripping wet. Weigh the damp sponge and record the result in your lab book.

5. Put the sponge in the water. Leave it for one minute, then measure and record how much of the sponge floats above the water.

6. Remove the sponge from the water and push in four panel pins. The heads of the panel pins should be almost level with the top of the sponge and they should be evenly spaced around it. Try not to squeeze out any water as you push in the panel pins. **Be careful not to stab yourself with the pointed ends**. Weigh the sponge with its panel pins and record the result.

7. Put the damp sponge with its panel pins into the water. Leave it for one minute, then measure and record its position in the water.

8. Carefully remove the sponge and push in four more panel pins in between the others. Weigh the sponge with its pins and record the result. Put the sponge with its panel pins back into the water. Leave it for one minute, then measure and record its position in the water.

9. Repeat step 8 until none of the sponge can float above the water, or you run out of panel pins.

Analysis of results

» Weigh the panel pins. How much weight could the damp sponge hold and still float?

» Did the sponge sink once it was full of nails? Why did this happen?

» Was the result what you expected?

More activities to extend your investigation

» Push panel pins through the sides of the sponge instead of the top and repeat the experiment.

» See if there is any difference when a bigger sponge is used, such as a car sponge.

» Float the sponge with the panel pins in another liquid and see if you get different results. For example, you could try soapy water or salty water.

» Instead of adding panel pins, try pouring small amounts of water onto the sponge. Use a kitchen measuring jug or measuring spoons so that you know how much water you have added. Can you sink the sponge with water alone?

Project extras

» Find out about life rafts and life jackets. What is the connection between your sponge and panel pins, and real life situations such as these? For example, a life raft crammed full of people is more likely to sink than an empty one, but what decides how many people it can hold safely?

MAERSK SEALAND

That sinking feeling

Why do some objects float while others sink? It has a lot to do with the **density** of the object. The more tightly packed the atoms and molecules are in an object, the denser it is. A dense object weighs a lot for its size. A less dense object contains a lot of air and is more likely to float. If it only has very tiny air pockets, down it goes! Keep that in mind as you do this investigation with your favourite foods.

Do your research

This investigation looks at whether or not an object floats or sinks, and the part that density plays in this. Before you begin your project, do some research to find out more about **buoyancy**, density, and how they're related, if at all. Once you've done this, you can tackle this investigation. Or, you might come up with an idea of your own after you've learned more about the topic.

Here are two websites you could start with for your research:

» Nova online: Buoyancy basics:
   http://www.pbs.org/wgbh/nova/lasalle/buoybasics.html
» How objects float in fluids:
   http://www.school-for-champions.com/science/fluidfloating.htm

Background information

Possible question

Which foods float the best in water?

Possible hypothesis

Light foods like bread will float better than heavy foods like apples.

Level of difficulty

Easy

Approximate cost of materials

Free to £5.00

Materials needed

» Eight different food items, such as apples, bread, meat, and so on.
» A large bucket or a washing up bowl
» A towel (to dry your hands and the working area)
» Kitchen scales (to find the weight of the food items)
» Stopwatch or watch

Outline of methods

1. Fill your bucket or bowl half full of clean water from the tap.

2. Prepare 50 g samples of eight different foods. It is wise to try to cut them all to the same shape, such as a cube. In your lab book, write your predictions about whether each food sample will float or sink.

3. Carefully put one of your food samples into the water. Wait for a second and decide if it is sinking or floating. Record the results in your lab book.

Step 3

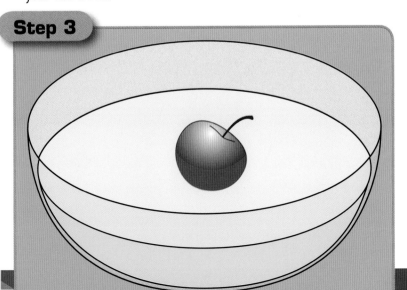

Continued

4. Use the watch to time one minute, then look at the food sample again. Is it floating or did it sink? Record the results again in your lab book.

5. Repeat steps 3 and 4 with each of the remaining food samples. Make sure you wash your hands thoroughly when you have finished. Do not eat your samples.

6. Chart your final results. Label the first column "Food" and make a list of the food samples used. Label the second column "Prediction" and write your prediction of whether it would float or sink. Next, make two wide columns labelled "One second" and "One minute." Under each of these headings, make two more columns, labelled "Floated" and "Sank."

    In a seventh column, write your notes about the food samples. Include what they are made of, what particular features of the foods affected their buoyancy, and how this helped you with your predictions.

Step 6

Food	Prediction	One Second		One Minute		Notes
		Floated	Sank	Floated	Sank	

Analysis of results

» After one second, which foods floated? Which foods sank?

» Did the result change after one minute had passed?

» Why do you think each food sample sank or didn't sink?

» If any of the foods floated, are there any similarities between them?

» If any of the food samples sank, are there any similarities between them?

» Were all the 50g pieces the same size? Did density affect their buoyancy?

These different types of food will keep you "afloat" during the day, but will they float in water?

More activities to extend your investigation

» Repeat the experiments using hot water or iced water.

» Try leaving the foods in the water for longer periods of time.

» Repeat the experiments using cooking oil instead of water. Which food samples do the same thing in water and oil, and which do something different?

» Choose the foods that sink. Time how long it takes for them to sink.

» Cook the food samples in a microwave oven or using boiling water in a pan (**ask permission and get an adult to work with you**). Does cooking make any difference to the buoyancy of a food sample?

Project extras

» Film your experiments or make a PowerPoint® presentation and show your class. Take photos to stick in your report.

Project antibubble

Some objects float because they have air pockets trapped inside them. Bubbles are air pockets that we can see. So it make sense that bubbles also float. But did you know there are **antibubbles** – air pockets you can see underwater? This is a tricky investigation, but well worth the effort. Will you master antibubbles?

Do your research

This investigation looks at **buoyancy**, the conditions needed to make antibubbles, and the properties of antibubbles. Before you start your investigation, do some research to find out more about antibubbles. Once you've done this, you can tackle this investigation. Or, you might come up with an idea of your own after you've learned more about the topic.

Here are two websites you could start with for your research:

» Antibubbles (Information about antibubbles with photos and videos):
http://antibubble.com
» More videos of antibubbles:
http://chemmovies.unl.edu/chemistry/beckerdemos/BD027.html

Background information

Possible question

How are antibubbles created?

Possible hypothesis:

Antibubbles are created when a liquid is inside a liquid.

Level of difficulty

Advanced

Approximate cost of materials

£8.00

Materials needed

» A large jug (it needs to hold at least 500 ml)
» A clear, tall, glass drinking tumbler
» A flat bowl (big enough for the glass to sit in it)
» A small cup or container
» A baby nasal decongester (in the chemist with the baby supplies)
» A paperclip
» Clear washing up liquid
» Table salt
» A tablespoon measuring spoon
» Camera (if you want to photograph your antibubbles)

Outline of methods

1. Make this mixture in your jug:

   450 ml of tap water
   2 pinches of salt
   2 tablespoons of washing up liquid

   Stir it slowly so that it doesn't get foamy (you want antibubbles, not bubbles!). Leave it overnight to clear the mixture.

2. The next day, stand the glass inside the bowl. Fill it to the brim with the mixture from step 1. Pour the rest into the small cup to use later. **Be careful when handling the glass and soapy mixture at the same time because the glass will be very slippery.**

3. Leave the mixture for 30 minutes to clear any foam.

 Continued

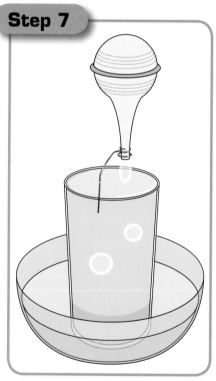

4. Straighten out the paperclip. Wrap it around the tip of the baby nasal decongester. Aim to have a metal "tail" sticking up beyond the end of the decongester. You have made a syringe.

5. Fill your syringe with some of the soapy mixture you saved in the cup in step 2. To do this, squeeze the bulb to push out the air, then dip the tip in the soapy mixture. Release the bulb. The syringe will fill up with the soapy mixture.

6. Hold the syringe just above the surface of the liquid in the glass tumbler. Make sure that the wire from the paperclip is dipping into the water. This is to stop static electricity bursting your antibubbles before they appear.

7. Gently squirt the soapy water from the syringe into the glass tumbler. Make sure the wire stays in the water. It may take some practice to make an antibubble. Start by squirting very gently, then more and more strongly until you see antibubbles forming. The antibubbles will look like normal bubbles, but with an extra layer inside. Remember from your research that antibubbles are liquid surrounded by a thin layer of air, inside another liquid.

8. Take photos of your antibubbles. They are very fragile and pop easily, so have your camera ready. If you have trouble making antibubbles that last long enough, you may want to find an assistant to take the pictures.

Analysis of results

» Were you able to make your own antibubbles? If so, what method worked best?

» What are antibubbles? What forces make them possible?

» Why do you think soapy water makes it easier to make antibubbles?

» What happens to the antibubbles when they burst?

» What would you change if you were to try this investigation again?

More activities to extend your investigation

» Add more salt to the soapy mixture that you inject with the syringe. This will make denser antibubbles that will sink to the bottom of the glass tumbler.

» Add food colouring to the soapy mixture you inject with the syringe. This will make coloured antibubbles.

» Add a layer of honey to the bottom of the glass before filling it with the soapy mixture. This will make the denser antibubbles last longer before bursting when they sink to the bottom.

Project extras:

» Film your experiments or make a PowerPoint® presentation about them and show your class. Stick the photos of your antibubbles into your report.

Writing your report

In many ways, writing the report of your investigation is the hardest part. You've researched the science involved, and you've had fun gathering all your evidence together. Now you have to explain what it's all about.

You are the expert

Very few other people, if any, will have done your investigation. So you are the expert here. You need to explain your ideas clearly. Scientists get their most important investigations published in a scientific magazine or journal. They may also stand up at meetings and tell other scientists what they have found. Or they may display a large poster to explain their investigation. You might consider giving a talk or making a poster about your investigation, too. But however scientists present their investigations, they always write it down first – and you must too. Here are some tips about what you should include in your report.

Some hints for collecting your results

» **Making a table:** Tables are great for recording lots of results. Use a pencil and ruler to draw your table lines, or make a table using a word processing program. Put the units (m, s, kg, N and so on) in the headings only. Don't write them into the main body of your table. Try to make your table fit one side of paper. If you need two sheets of paper, make sure you write the column headings on the second sheet as well.

» **Recording your results:** It is often easy to forget to write down your results as they come in. Or you might just scribble them onto the back of your hand, and then wash your hands! A wise scientist will always make a neat, blank table in their lab book before starting. They will write down their results as they go along and not later on.

» **Odd stuff:** If something goes wrong, make a note of it. This will remind you which results might not be reliable.

» **Precision:** Always record your readings to the precision of your measuring equipment. For example, if you have scales that show 24.6 g, don't write 24 or 25 in your table. Instead, write 24.6 because that's the precise measurement.

Laying out your report

You could use the following headings to organise your report in a clear manner:

» **A title**

This gives an idea of what your investigation is about.

» **Aims**

Write a brief outline of what you were trying to do. It should include the question you were trying to answer.

» **Hypothesis**

This is your scientific prediction of what will happen in your investigation. Include notes from your research to explain why you think your prediction will work out. It might help to write it out as: "I think … will happen because …"

» **Materials**

List the equipment you used to carry out your experiments. Also say what any measuring equipment was for. For example, "scales (to weigh the objects)".

» **Methods**

Explain what you actually did in your investigation.

» **Results**

Record your results, readings, and observations clearly.

» **Conclusions**

Explain how closely your results fitted your hypothesis. You can find out more about this on the next page.

» **Bibliography**

List the books, articles, websites, or other resources you used in your research.

And finally ... the conclusions

There are two main bits to your conclusions. These are the "Analysis" and the "Evaluation". In the analysis you explain what your evidence shows, and how it supports or disproves your **hypothesis**. In the evaluation, you discuss the quality of your results and their reliability, and how successful your methods were.

Your analysis

You need to study your **evidence** to see if there is a relationship between the **variables** in your investigation. This can be difficult to spot in a table, so it is a good idea to draw a graph. You should always put the **dependent variable** on the vertical axis, and the **independent variable** on the horizontal axis. The type of graph you need to draw depends on the type of variables involved:

» A bar chart if the results are **categoric**, such as hot/cold, male/female.
» A line graph or a scattergram if both variables are **continuous**, such as time, length, or mass.

Remember to label the axes to say what each one shows, and the unit used. For example, "time in s" or "height in cm". Draw a line or curve of best fit if you can.

Explain what your graph shows. Remember that the reader needs help from you to understand your investigation. Even if you have spotted a pattern, don't assume that your reader has. Tell them. For example, "My graph shows that the higher up the ball was dropped, the higher it bounced". Circle any points on your graph that seem **anomalous** (too high or too low).

Your evaluation

Did your investigation go well, or did it go badly? Was your evidence good enough for you to support or disprove your hypothesis? Sometimes it can be difficult for you to answer these questions. But it is really important that you try. Scientists always look back at their investigations. They want to know if they could improve their methods next time. They also want to know if their evidence is **reliable** and **valid**. Reliable evidence can be repeated with pretty much the same results. Valid evidence is reliable, and it should answer the question you asked in the first place. As before, remember that you are the person who knows your investigation the best. Don't be afraid to show off valid evidence. And be honest if it's not!

Glossary

acceleration increase in speed

accurate close to the true value

aerodynamics the study of how objects move through the air

air resistance drag on an object as it moves through the air

anomalous a result that seems out of place, such as too high or too low

antibubble a droplet of liquid surrounded by a thin film of air inside another liquid

buoyancy ability to float

categoric a variable that can be given labels, such as male/female

continuous a variable that can have any value, such as weight or length

control something that is left unchanged in order to compare results against it

data measurements or observations made in an experiment

density the mass of an object divided by its volume

dependent variable the variable that changes because of what you do in an experiment

diameter distance through the centre of an object from one side to the other

evidence data that has been checked to see if it is valid

gravity force that attracts objects to the centre of the Earth

hypothesis an idea about why something happens that can be tested by experiments

independent variable a variable that you deliberately keep the same or change in an experiment

mass amount of matter in a material or object

newton (N) unit of force

prediction what you think will happen, in advance, based on a scientific idea

reliable results that can be repeated

valid valid results come from a fair test

variable something that changes or can be changed

weight the amount of force acting on an object because of its mass and the Earth's gravity

Index